NO SUCH COLD THING

Naomi Wallace

BROADWAY PLAY PUBLISHING INC
224 E 62nd St, NY, NY 10065
www.broadwayplaypub.com
info@broadwayplaypub.com

NO SUCH COLD THING
© Copyright 2016 by Naomi Wallace

First printing: July 2016
I S B N: 978-0-88145-653-0

Book design: Marie Donovan
Typographic controls: Adobe InDesign
Typeface: Palatino
Printed and bound in the U S A

NO SUCH COLD THING was commissioned by the Tricycle Theater of London in 2008, as part of *The Great Game: Afghanistan*.

The play received its world premiere at the ReOrient 2009 Festival, produced by Gold Thread Productions and directed by Bella Ramazan-Nia.

CHARACTERS

MEENA, *a young Afghan, 15 years of age*
ALYA, *a young Afghan, 13 years of age*
SERGIO, *U S Army soldier, Chicano, twenties*

Time: Late Autumn, 2001

Place: Just outside Sar Asia at the edge of a possible desert, near Kabul, Afghanistan.

"Grief melts away
Like snow in May,
As if there were no such cold thing."
—George Herbert

(Lights up on an almost empty stage/desert. Night. Two sandbags, one slightly smaller than the other, lie upstage, some distance apart. ALYA, *wearing a burka, stands center stage, looking up into the sky. She carries a small, hard, old fashioned suitcase. Suddenly her sister* MEENA *appears.* MEENA *is wearing a headscarf covering her hair, and a long coat, covering her more Western-style dress.* ALYA *is startled to see* MEENA. *They stare at one another for some moments in silence.)*

MEENA: Hedge hog? Is it you, hedge hog? Alya, is it you?

ALYA: *(Quotes)* "He is the lord of sleep/lord of peace/lord of night."

MEENA: *(Quotes)* "on whose arm your hair is lying" *(She claps her hands with joy.)* You still have a good memory for verse!

ALYA: Ahmed Faiz gets sentimental when it comes to his Lord. Allah doesn't like sentiment. He prefers lemons, hard rain and hedge hogs.

*(*MEENA *takes a small book of verse from her coat.)*

MEENA: I've still got the book.

*(*MEENA *holds it out to* ALYA *but she doesn't take it.)*

ALYA: You stole it when you left. That was our one book of verse that Uncle Khan brought back from his studies in Pakistan.

MEENA: What do you care if I took it? You don't like Faiz.

ALYA: But I like to read. Mother taught us from that book.

MEENA: Show me your face.

ALYA: Not here. I'm not supposed to be out of the house.

MEENA: Look at my hair.

(MEENA *pulls her scarf off and shakes her hair free.* ALYA *gasps and looks about her nervously.*)

ALYA: I can see your ankles. They'll kill you.

MEENA: They're on the run. The Americans have sent them running.

ALYA: Not all of them are running.

MEENA: Let me see your ankles.

ALYA: *(Backing away)* No.

MEENA: Please.

ALYA: It is forbidden.

MEENA: Let me see your hair.

(ALYA *shakes her head "no".*)

MEENA: All right. But I can see your shape through the cloth. The little hedge hog has become a woman. *(Beat)* That's your suitcase then? It's not much. I've so many things now I'd need six suitcases! But we have to go. The taxi is waiting at the end of the road.

ALYA: We have no one to travel with us. If the Taliban see us travelling alone, they'll beat us.

MEENA: I told you they've left the area. It's all clear.

(MEENA *moves to take* ALYA's *suitcase but* ALYA *won't let it go.*)

ALYA: I can't go to England with you.

MEENA: Don't be silly. Father is waiting for us at the airport. They wouldn't let him pass but he is waiting. The airport is in the hands of the Americans. It's safe.

ALYA: I can't speak English. They'll laugh at me.

MEENA: You're speaking English now.

ALYA: Mother still pulls me out of bed at 2 A M. I try to bite her because I am so tired. We do math, geometry, English.

MEENA: If my exams are good I'll go to University. I'm going to write a brilliant essay on Faiz Ahmed Faiz and—

ALYA: the idea of hell and heaven. You already wrote us about that.

MEENA: Oh. *(Beat.)* The taxi won't wait for long. He warned me. Father is anxious.

ALYA: Mother says she'll follow us soon. I don't believe her. She limps. In England they won't like a limp.

MEENA: Don't be stupid, everyone limps in England.

(ALYA suddenly eyes MEENA.)

ALYA: You've lost your tarbia.

MEENA: No. I haven't lost my manners.

ALYA: You go without the burka.

MEENA: In England no one cares. I wear the hijab. Sometimes just a scarf. Father agrees.

ALYA: What size bra do you wear now? When you left you only had buds. I see melons now.

MEENA: *(Delighted)* Not melons. Maybe oranges, yes. But I think yours are bigger and I'm older than you! Can I see them?

ALYA: No. Do you let men touch you?

MEENA: Of course not. But I make a noise when I walk.

(MEENA *opens her coat and walks in a circle, purposely clicking her heels as she walks.* ALYA *is nervous.*)

ALYA: Shhh. Shhhh. Someone will hear you.

(MEENA *just laughs and makes louder clicks as she walks.*)

ALYA: Remember Fauzia?

MEENA: Fauzia with the black, black hair.

ALYA: Black as oil.

MEENA: I think I'm prettier than she is now.

ALYA: Fauzia was walking with her father to see family. It was two years ago. She had on her best shoes and they made a click, click, click. Not loud but too loud. The Virtue Police heard Fauzia clicking and they beat her.

(ALYA *watches* MEENA *walk. Then* MEENA *stops "clicking".*)

ALYA: Its true. Now you are prettier than she was.

MEENA: Let's go.

ALYA: We've been alone, mother and I, and outside, the Taliban. We cannot leave the house. Mother had to stop her teaching; she is forbidden to work. Uncle Khan keeps us alive with scraps from his table. Our cousin Nargis laughed too loud at the market and the Virtue Police hit her and now she is missing three front teeth and is ugly. Girls are not allowed to go outside at all. I'm forbidden to learn to read and write. There is no one to collect the water. Uncle brings it. And all this. All this and you and father are far away in England, clicking.

MEENA: The plan was for Father and I to get out first. You know that. We couldn't get back here 'til now.

ALYA: *(Calmly)* Pig. I want to slap you.

(MEENA *steps close to* ALYA, *within her reach.*)

MEENA: Then slap me.

(ALYA *and* MEENA *just regard one another.*)

ALYA: Does it rain in England all the time?

MEENA: It rains. But it's not hard rain.

ALYA: Then Allah doesn't like England. Will you take me to buy earrings?

MEENA: Yes.

ALYA: Mother says they have hedgehogs there. But with little ears, not like here with the long ears.

MEENA: You can buy a bird at a shop on the high street and teach it to sit on your finger.

ALYA: Do the English like their hedge hogs?

MEENA: There is a hedge hog society. You can join.

ALYA: But they'll laugh at me. All the children in the new school will laugh at me.

MEENA: You're just a girl. That's not so funny. No one will laugh.

ALYA: Liar. I'm not just a girl. My back hurts. It hurts so much I can hardly move.

MEENA: What's wrong with your back?

ALYA: Quills. I'm growing quills.

(MEENA *laughs but* ALYA *is serious.*)

ALYA: Along my spine.

MEENA: Let me see.

(MEENA *grabs at* ALYA *but* ALYA *dodges her.*)

ALYA: No! You might cut yourself. The quills are sharp. I can't go with you.

MEENA: You're just scared. Take my hand.

(MEENA *holds out her hand but* ALYA *doesn't take it.*)

ALYA: Don't tell anyone. It's a secret. *(She thinks she hears something, whispers.)* Shhh. Footsteps!

(ALYA and MEENA both listen, alert.)

MEENA: It's nothing. The streets are clear tonight. We're safe. Alya, I have a secret too.

ALYA: Tell me.

MEENA: I've been held in the arms. Of a man.

(ALYA slaps MEENA's face. MEENA touches the sting with her hand.)

ALYA: You are dirty. You are disrespectful. You shame me. You shame father.

(MEENA just stares at ALYA.)

ALYA: Tell me more.

MEENA: It was night. Dark. I couldn't find my way home. I got lost. Such a big city. I was tired and he put his arms around me, and carried me.

ALYA: *(Eager)* Did he squeeze your boobs?

MEENA: Now you are dirty! No. He just carried me and then put me down again. His hands were warm. He touched my neck.

ALYA: You've been touched by a man not of your family. That's a death sentence for you here. Whore. Whore. I have missed you every hour. I smell your clothes to remember you. Your bed is silent and your pencil cold on the table. *(Beat)* We'll come back here when we're teachers?

MEENA: Yes. And we'll teach in the daylight. And girls will be allowed to go to school.

ALYA: And we'll scrape, scrape the paint from the windows.

MEENA: And we'll open our doors, skip out any time,

ALYA: and we won't need a man to be with us.

MEENA: And we can click and shout as loud as…

ALYA: cannons! And we can eat till our bellies are round…

MEENA: as buckets!

ALYA: And we'll have radio and singing

MEENA: and so many apples we can fill our mouths…

ALYA: till they burst!

(ALYA *and* MEENA *are enjoying their reunion, but then suddenly they find their composure again.* ALYA *glances around nervously, fearing their discovery.*)

ALYA: Shhhh. Okay. I'm ready to go with you, sister. My back hurts and I can't move but my shoes are strong.

(MEENA *notices now that* ALYA*'s shoe lace is hanging loose.*)

MEENA: Your shoe lace is untied. Let me tie it.

(ALYA *doesn't move for a moment. Then she slowly lifts the hem of her burka to reveal that she is wearing U S Army boots, far too big for her.*)

MEENA: Oh my.

ALYA: That's what I said when I found them. But at least they're warm on my feet.

(ALYA *and* MEENA *continue to stare at* ALYA*'s shoes. Elsewhere on stage* SERGIO *wakes on a small bed that has no mattress. He's been sleeping on the springs but he doesn't seem to notice. A sand bag is his pillow. The bed is rusty and old. He is wearing boxer shorts and is barefoot. He shakes his head and moans, confused.*)

SERGIO: Fuckin' Kubick. Jeez that guy can put 'em away. Put 'em away. Kubick. And Tony, and Mike,

and… Shit. We were all there at…Joe's Place, yeah
bunch of drunks and I didn't even drink that much.

(SERGIO's *words roll steady out of him.*)

SERGIO: And I said I'm going to have one of those dogs
Yeah I'm going to eat one of those dogs That one Yeah
I was hungry and my gut hurt. I'm still hungry and my
gut hurts. Mama's gonna make me french toast when
she gets up. What time is it?…

(SERGIO *rubs his head and eyes.*)

SERGIO: Give me one of those jumbo-sized hot dogs
I said last night they all laughed Fuck you I said and
your mother and your sister even if she is only ten
the hot dogs were turnin' and turnin' the heat lamp
burnin' them almost black and then. She was there,
alone at the bar.

(SERGIO *runs his hands out along what he thinks is a
mattress.*)

SERGIO: And she was so pretty and her mouth was…
Her hair was so…Her neck was so… What? What? I
can't remember. Her hair was… Her mouth was… And
then she was gone.

(SERGIO *suddenly feels the metal of the springs. He jumps
up.*)

SERGIO: What the…fuck—

(SERGIO *suddenly looks around him and then under the
bed. He finds his pyjamas and starts to put them on. He still
seems to be missing something.*)

SERGIO: Shit where are they? Where are they? *(Shouts)*
Must have been one hell of a night hell of a night at
Joe's Place.

(SERGIO *is now dressed in his pyjamas. He surveys his bed.
He notices something odd about his pillow. He takes a closer
look.*)

SERGIO: Kubick, Tony, Mike and…

(SERGIO *discovers that the pillow is a sandbag. He pulls it off the bed and holds it, his arms out stretched. It strains him to hold it like this.*)

SERGIO: Fuck this for a pillow. *(Calls out)* Mama? Mama you up yet?

(*Hearing no answer from his mother,* SERGIO *flings the sandbag away. It lands at the feet of* ALYA *and* MEENA. *Now the girls look at the "pillow" that has landed between them. Then they simultaneously see* SERGIO *and he sees them.*)

SERGIO: God damn! *(He speaks in a rush of words to the sisters.)* I wasn't I forgot I didn't I'm sorry but I must have been too drunk but hey it's all right it's all right. *(Beat)* Two, huh. Two of you? Man I must have been wasted cause I can't remember picking you up. I can't remember bringing no chick home. Chicks home.

MEENA: We are sisters.

SERGIO: Hermanas. Jesus, sisters. *(Laughs)* Wait till I tell Kubick, Tony, Mike and. They won't believe it. *(He notes* ALYA's *suitcase.)* Uh. I guess you need a ride home?

ALYA: We have a taxi, thank you.

MEENA: Waiting at the end of the road.

SERGIO: Great. Cause I don't got a car. *(He looks hard at* MEENA.) Now you I kinda remember your face. *(He looks at* ALYA *in her burka.)* Don't suppose I'd remember yours anyway. But hey, to each his own. To each his own, yeah.

ALYA: The airport is safe now? Meena says its safe?

SERGIO: Last time I checked. I flew Delta home. Did my Mama see you come in last night?

(ALYA *and* MEENA *are confused by his question but shake their heads "no".*)

SERGIO: Good. Good. I mean my Mama she's open minded and she knows I got needs but she just doesn't want me fillin them in her house. How 'bout you go out the back door?

(ALYA *looks around perplexed.*)

MEENA: We're going to England.

ALYA: We're going to get our diplomas.

SERGIO: Even better, would you mind going out the window? I think the back door's locked.

(ALYA *and* MEENA *glance around, uncertain.*)

ALYA: Where is your uniform, soldier?

SERGIO: Mama has it at the dry cleaners. Hey, hope you don't mind but I forgot your names.

MEENA: I am Meena. This is my sister, Alya.

ALYA: Put on your uniform please. We are young women. We don't want to see your feet.

SERGIO: You want me in my uniform? A little kink? I like a little kink. We going to do it again then?

ALYA: Do what again?

(SERGIO *just grins.*)

SERGIO: Sisters, huh? I never did two at a time before. How did I do?

MEENA: Where is your gun?

SERGIO: I mean you came home with me so you must think I'm hot.

ALYA: Where is your helmet?

SERGIO: I mean I kinda hope you think I'm a little bit hot...

MEENA: How many Taliban did you kill today?

SERGIO: Hey. Don't get personal.

ALYA: Can you read?

MEENA: Can you write?

SERGIO: What do you think? A year at the U of Indiana but then I joined. Thought they'd make me a pilot. Ha. No fucking luck cause they put me on the ground.

MEENA: But you're American.

(SERGIO *now really looks at* ALYA *and* MEENA *for the first time, as though his hangover is clearing.*)

ALYA: We'll be able to work now. We'll be able to read and write

MEENA: and calculate, because of you.

ALYA: But if they see Meena's hair they will kill her.

SERGIO: *(To* ALYA*)* Let me see your face, honey.

(ALYA *steps back.*)

SERGIO: Come on. I seen more than that last night.

(MEENA *steps in front of* ALYA.*)

MEENA: Pick up your suitcase, sister. We must go now.

(ALYA *emits a sharp scream, and puts her hands to her back. Then she's just as suddenly still.*)

SERGIO: *(Panicked)* Shush. Shush. Shush. Shush. Shit.

ALYA: My back hurts.

SERGIO: If my Mama hears you and comes in here, I am fuckin' toast. Out the window. Both of you. Now.

(ALYA *and* MEENA *both look around.*)

MEENA: What window?

SERGIO: The only fuckin' window in my bedroom.

ALYA: There is no window. Do you have quills?

SERGIO: What?

ALYA: Quills.

SERGIO: No, no, no. I don't do the hard stuff. A little dope. Jack on the weekends. But no quills.

ALYA: They're growing on my back.

MEENA: You said it was a secret.

ALYA: He's just an American. He won't tell anyone. Will you?

(SERGIO *is uncertain but shakes his head "no".*)

SERGIO: Where you girls from?

ALYA: We were born here.

MEENA: Our father was born here. And his father's father.

SERGIO: Huh.

ALYA: Same piece of land.

MEENA: Grapes, mulberries, pomegranates.

SERGIO: Pomegranates? Shit. You grow pomegranates here?

MEENA: Our pomegranates are famous in India and Iran.

SERGIO: Bullshit, chica. Only thing that grows in Gary, Indiana is unemployment.

ALYA: Who is Gary Indiana?

MEENA: *(To* ALYA*)* I think it's a movie about temples of doom. *(To* SERGIO*)* Are you married?

SERGIO: No…

MEENA: Engaged?

SERGIO: No… Now wait just a minute. If you two are trying to trick me it won't work. I use a wrapper.

When I hose a girl I wrap up real tight so no babies. No babies from me.

ALYA: *(Looking at* SERGIO's *toes.)* Oh my. Its a shame to say it but you have ugly toes. Doesn't he, Meena?

MEENA: Well, they're almost as ugly as Uncle Khan's.

(All three look at SERGIO's *feet.)*

SERGIO: Well, I'm sorry about the feet but last night, as you most likely remember, I lost my boots.

ALYA: I don't think you are a good soldier.

SERGIO: You watch your mouth. I did my service. Got a purple pulling a buddy out under fire.

MEENA: You shouldn't lose your boots. It's bad luck.

SERGIO: Shit.

MEENA: Don't you like being a soldier?

SERGIO: I didn't say that. Army's paying me to finish school. I started last week. I'd lick their ass if they ran out of toilet paper.

ALYA: You have bad tarbia.

MEENA: She means manners. A man without good tarbia won't find a wife.

SERGIO: Great. 'Cause honey I don't want to get hitched. Certainly to neither of you.

ALYA: They you're still chaste?

SERGIO: Yeah. Chaste as the fuckin' dew.

MEENA: That's my favourite verse in the book, "There's no dew/anywhere, so/strange that there's no dew/anywhere"

ALYA: *(Quotes)* "not on the forehead/of the cold sun,"

SERGIO: Huh?

ALYA: She's got a thing for Faiz Ahmed Faiz.

SERGIO: Well if he thinks he can move in on my chick, my chicks, without talking to me first, I'll take out his lights.

MEENA: *(Quotes)* "And the roses of your hands, the—"

ALYA: *(Quotes)* "the decanter and the glass,/were like the outline/of a dream.'

SERGIO: *(To* ALYA*)* Baby, baby.

MEENA: *(Stomps her foot)* Stop doing that, Alya.

ALYA: What?

SERGIO: I like the way you talk to me.

MEENA: Finishing the lines. I hate it.

(ALYA *sticks her tongue at* MEENA *and continues.)*

MEENA: Stupid Hedgehog.

ALYA: See, I'm not even in England yet and already they're calling me names.

SERGIO: Who's calling you names?

ALYA: *(To* SERGIO*)* Everyone. Because of my quills. Down my spine, I only have three hundred of them. But the hedgehog has seven thousand. I have a long way to go. They're ugly but I need them. They're not solid, the quills. Each one is filled with a complex network of chambers, so they're lightweight and strong, so they won't buckle and break.

MEENA: *(To* SERGIO*)* All she knows is about those quills. *(To* ALYA*)* You ignorant brat.

(While ALYA *and* MEENA *face off,* SERGIO *moves around the stage curiously, uncertain now as to his surroundings.)*

ALYA: You shit English girl who leaves her sister and mother behind, with nothing but a fart and a smile.

MEENA: You're right. They won't like you in England. Your mouth is full of dirt.

ALYA: Your head is full of worms.
You left us to rot. Father left us to rot.

MEENA: I'll pull out your hair.

(ALYA *and* MEENA *raise their fists at each other, ready to fight.*)

ALYA: I'll tell the village you're a whore.

MEENA: I'll tear out your quills!

(*Suddenly* SERGIO *is between* ALYA *and* MEENA, *pushing them apart.*)

SERGIO: Stop it! Both of you. There will be no ass-kicking in my space. You should be ashamed.

(ALYA *and* MEENA *quit, but turn their backs to one another.*)

SERGIO: You don't fight family.

(ALYA *and* MEENA *remain with their backs to eachother, angry.*)

SERGIO: Hey. Hey! You two make up now.

ALYA/MEENA: Never!

SERGIO: Listen you guys. When its la familia. The family. You never say never.

(SERGIO *takes* ALYA's *hand. She tries to pull away but he holds on. She calms. Then he takes* MEENA's *hand.* MEENA *resists less but its still strange to hold a man's hand.* SERGIO *squashes the sister's hands together.*)

SERGIO: Because when there's no one else there anymore. Not even a sound. Nothing. Nada...

(*For a short moment all three of them are holding hands but then* SERGIO *quickly lets go, uncomfortable.*)

SERGIO: Okay, you two are good again? Right.

(ALYA *and* MEENA *glance furtively at each other and nod.*)

SERGIO: So as Rafael Nadal the king of clay would say: Vamos. As Sergio Vasquez, that's me, would say as nicely as possible: Please, Get. The. Hell. Out. Of. My. House. Now.

ALYA: We're not in your house. How dare you suggest it? This is a desert.

SERGIO: Well, yeah, there's not much here sure, but who needs more than a bed, right?

ALYA: Let's go, Meena. I don't like his mouth.

(ALYA *turns to leave.* MEENA *is reluctant.*)

MEENA: But Alya, we must have compassion for his bad tarbia.

SERGIO: Sure, whatever. Just get going now and haul ass out my window. (*He looks around but can no longer see his window.*) Hey. Where's my window?

ALYA: In our home we had to paint the windows because it's forbidden for men to look inside the house and see us.

SERGIO: It was right here. (*He is disorientated.*)

MEENA: This is the desert. We are in the desert.

ALYA: Bye, bye soldier.

SERGIO: I could see the oak tree from my bed.

MEENA: There are no trees here.

SERGIO: Hey, where the hell am I?

ALYA: I don't think I like you. Do you like him, Meena?

MEENA: Only a little. Maybe. But I'm glad we won't have to look at his toes anymore.

ALYA: Let's go then. But Meena, my other shoe lace is untied. Help me.

(MEENA *bends down to tie* ALYA's *other shoe lace.* ALYA *lifts the hem of her burka.* SERGIO *sees his boots.*)

SERGIO: Hey. Those are my boots!

MEENA: Don't be stupid.

SERGIO: I been lookin' for them all over.

ALYA: Finders keepers.

SERGIO: That's U S Army property.

ALYA: Not anymore.

SERGIO: Where did you get them?

MEENA: *(Finishes tying.)* Good-bye, Soldier.

ALYA: *(Chants to SERGIO)*
Watch your back. Watch your back.
Taliban, Taliban might come back!

(MEENA makes a "whooo" scary sound, then ALYA continues chanting at SERGIO, taunting him.)

ALYA: Taliban, Taliban,Taliban
Come to chew you
Come to swallow you

(ALYA and MEENA laugh and chant together, staggerring the song, as though this song were their childhood 'row, row, row the boat', but far darker.)

ALYA/MEENA: Taliban, taliban, taliban
Will take your eyes
And make apple pies.

(ALYA and MEENA move to leave. SERGIO purposely steps on the hem of ALYA's burka to stop her. ALYA can't walk further. She strains against the cloth to walk forward but can't. He picks up the hem and slowly pulls the burka off of ALYA. When ALYA is revealed, it is as though she is waking from a dream. ALYA is dressed in slacks and a long sleeved shirt. She looks down at her "nakedness" and as she kneels she cries out in fright, as though she is falling.)

(MEENA rushes to her side but its as though ALYA can't see her.)

MEENA: Alya? What is it? Alya?

(*Now* ALYA *begins to chant again, as though to comfort herself.*)

ALYA: *(Whispers)* Will come to chew you
Come to swallow you.

MEENA: Alya!

ALYA: *(Chants)* Will take your eyes
and make apple pies.

SERGIO: Don't ever separate a man from his boots.

(SERGIO *moves to pull the boots off of* ALYA's *feet but* MEENA *gets there first and takes the boots.* ALYA *does not resist.* MEENA *clutches the boots to her chest defiantly.* SERGIO *moves towards her, she evades him.*)

ALYA/MEENA: *(Chant)* They'll slip into your home
and eat you to the bone

SERGIO: Come on, honey. Don't tease me.

ALYA/MEENA: *(Chant)* They'll slip into your bed
and hump you till you're.

(ALYA *finishes the chant by herself, now alert to her surroundings.*)

ALYA: Dead. Dead. *(Beat)* Dead.

(MEENA *turns and starts to walk away.* SERGIO *no longer acts like he's in pyjama's but in a battle zone. He flips the bed on its side so its a barrier he's standing behind. He starts out speaking calmly but then gets more frenzied.*)

SERGIO: Stay where you are. All of you. Hey. Get back in line. That's right. Get back in line. Hey. Stop right there, kid. Hey. I mean you.

(SERGIO *has no gun but he seems to be holding something in his arms, perhaps the memory of a gun. All the while he shouts at* MEENA, *she keeps slowly walking away.*)

SERGIO: Stop. I'm warning you. I'm warning you! You stop. You stop! Hey. Fucking stop or I shoot!

(MEENA *now stops walking and stands very still for some moments. As though she were suspended. Then she turns around and looks first at* SERGIO, *then at* ALYA. *The boots fall from her arms.*)

ALYA: Soldier, soldier.

(SERGIO *comes out of his "state", and looks himself over.*)

SERGIO: I don't have a gun.

ALYA: But he did today.

MEENA: *(To* ALYA*)* Where, Alya?

ALYA: In the yard.

MEENA: Where on my body do you think he shot me?

ALYA: In your neck.

SERGIO: No, no, no. *(He violently kicks the bed out of the way.)* I fucked you I didn't shoot you. Right here in my bedroom.

(ALYA *and* MEENA *ignore* SERGIO.)

MEENA: I don't believe you, Alya.

ALYA: Okay.

SERGIO: Well you better believe me.

MEENA: This is one of your stupid tricks, hedgehog. Isn't it?

SERGIO: Yeah. This is one of her stupid tricks. I got drunk last night. In my home town bar. In Gary. In Indiana. With Kubick, Tony, Mike and. With Kubick, Tony, Mike and... *(Shouts)* Mamma? Wake up. Come in here!

ALYA: *(To* SERGIO, *calmly)* Meena was running in the yard. Everyone was standing in line. You told us to stand in line.

SERGIO: Be quiet. *(Calls)* Mama!

ALYA: There were twenty of you, maybe thirty. We raised our arms. My mother, my father.

SERGIO: *(Calls)* Hey!

ALYA: My father's arms were trembling and he was ashamed so he raised his arms higher. And you were in command.

SERGIO: You're out of your mind.

ALYA: You said

SERGIO: *(In Dari)* Raise your arms. Don't move.

ALYA: *(Translating)* Raise your arms. All of you. Don't move.

(MEENA raises her arms in the air.)

SERGIO: *(In Dari)* And keep them up or we'll shoot.

ALYA: *(Translating)* And keep them up or we'll shoot. *(She looks at* MEENA *as she speaks.)* Meena broke out of the line and ran.

SERGIO: I told her to stop.

ALYA: She didn't stop.

SERGIO: I was scared.

ALYA: She was scared.

SERGIO: *(To himself)* Fuck.

(While ALYA *and* MEENA *continue to speak,* SERGIO *very quietly talks to himself and to his mother in Spanish as he sits on the bed, gets up, sits again, trying to force himself into another reality, trying to make himself believe he is at home.)*

MEENA: I was afraid. Because… *(She slowly lowers her arms, trying to remember.)*

ALYA: You were afraid because I broke out of the line.
I ran so fast the soldiers couldn't stop me. I ran round
the back of the house.

MEENA: You ran round the back of the house?

ALYA: I could not breathe. *(Beat)* I cannot breathe.
Father tells us not to move. Mother is shushing us.
All of us in line. The whole village. You grip my hand
so tight, so tight and tell me to be still. You hum my
favorite song to keep me quiet. *(She hums a line of the
song MEENA hummed to her.)* That's how it goes. But
your throat is dry with fear and the tune will not
come out. So I pull. I pull and pull til my hand comes
out from your hand. And then I run. I run so fast you
almost can't see me. But I trip and fall, down the well.
And as I fall I grow quills so quick because while
hedgehogs are skilled climbers, they are not so good at
getting down. When they come across a drop they roll
into a ball and just. Drop. The quills cushion the fall. To
keep the quills from being damaged, the thin stem just
above the skin flexes on impact. Wild hedge hogs have
been seen to drop twenty feet with no apparent signs
of injury. *(Beat)* Down the well I fall and when I hit the
bottom, because I don't have enough quills, my back
breaks. Crack. I cannot move. I lie on my back in three
inches of water.

MEENA: *(Remembering)* You ran first. Yes. I was afraid
for you so I ran after you. Didn't I?

(ALYA doesn't answer.)

MEENA: *(Shouts)* Didn't I?

ALYA: Yes.

MEENA: So it's your fault I got shot.

ALYA: I had to run. I couldn't stand still.

MEENA: *(Angry)* It's your fault. It's your fault! You let
my hand go.

ALYA: From where I lay on my back in the well I could see a round circle of sky above me. *(To* SERGIO.*)* And then I heard you fire. And then I heard my sister—

SERGIO: *(Interrupts, to* ALYA*)* I gave her warning. I gave her half a dozen warnings. But she kept on running. She dropped so fast to the ground. I couldn't believe how fast she dropped. I knelt beside her. I picked her up and carried her into the shade.

MEENA: You carried me?

SERGIO: Yes.

MEENA: How?

SERGIO: How? What the hell does it matter?

MEENA: It matters to me. It matters to me!

*(*SERGIO *looks around, locates a sandbag and picks it up in his arms. He adjusts his arms to hold the sand bag better.)*

MEENA: You held me in your arms like that?

SERGIO: Yeah.

ALYA: He touched your neck.

MEENA: *(To* SERGIO*)* You touched my neck?

SERGIO: I tried to stop the bleeding but

ALYA: there was too much of it.

SERGIO: There was too much of it. I'd never shot someone before. Your neck was so small and. So small and. My bullet was in there. My bullet was in there, inside, and I couldn't get it out. I couldn't get it out. Your skin. Your skin was so—

ALYA: *(Interrupts)* Don't you shame my sister!

SERGIO: Your mouth was so—

ALYA: *(Interrupts)* Don't you talk about Meena like that.

MEENA: Let him speak.

SERGIO: Your hair lay across my arm, black and—

ALYA: Shut your mouth!

MEENA: Alya, please!

SERGIO: Your hair lay across my arm, black and...

MEENA: My hair was black and what? What, soldier?

(SERGIO *now turns away and will not answer.*)

MEENA: My mouth was what? Speak! My skin was what?

(SERGIO *can no longer remember. For a moment he just looks at* MEENA.)

SERGIO: You were alive when I carried you.

(MEENA *and* SERGIO *regard one another.*)

MEENA: I was alive? (*To* ALYA) He says I was alive, Alya, so I didn't die. I didn't die!

ALYA: You are alive, Meena. Right now. For a few more minutes. And I am alive for this same time. And the soldier too. For a few more minutes.

SERGIO: Hey. Hey. This is your shit, don't bring me into it. I got out. I got out.

ALYA: Yes. You and your buddies get out. You get out fast because the Taliban have circled back and Kubick, Tony and Mike are with you and you're gunning the truck and spinning away from our village and then BANG, guess what?

SERGIO: Guess what? Guess fucking what? I'm going back to bed. I ate a hot dog long as a my leg last night.

ALYA: Indigestion.

SERGIO: Like you wouldn't believe.

ALYA: (*Loud*) Bang!

SERGIO: I'm going back to sleep.

ALYA: *(Louder)* Bang!

SERGIO: I was out drinking last night. With Kubick, Tony, Mike and. Kubick, Tony, Mike and.

ALYA: You. Kubick, Tony, Mike and you. Hit a land mine. Your friends are unharmed but you fly up in the air, high, high and your boots fly off your feet, one with a foot still attached and Uncle sees your boots lying a hundred feet from your body. He throws your boots in the well to hide them. He is afraid the village will be blamed. He doesn't even know I'm down there.

SERGIO: *(Threatening)* You are a dirty girl.

ALYA: Yes. At this very moment I am covered in dirt and slime at the bottom of a well and I'm dying. And my sister Meena is in the yard and she is also dying. And you are lying on the road and Kubick, Tony and Mike are leaning over you and you are dying.

SERGIO: *(Fiercely)* No. No way. I'm in bed.

ALYA: *(Shrugs)* I think we got caught in each other's …

SERGIO: *(Interrupts)* I'm in bed and my mothers making french toast in the kitchen and I can smell it burnin at the edges, just the way I like it.

(ALYA starts to laugh. She laughs and laughs. Then she points to the largest sand bag.)

SERGIO: And I'm in my pyjamas. I'm in my pyjamas. *(Shouts)* I'm in my fucking pyjamas and I'm home. In Gary, Indiana. I made it home!

(Now they are all silent some moments. ALYA just stares at SERGIO till he looks away. Now he knows he didn't make it home.)

MEENA: *(Quietly)* Alya, I'm sorry to say this but you are a liar. I went to England. I studied Faiz Ahmed Faiz.

ALYA: You didn't go to England. We can't even speak English.

MEENA: But we are speaking English.

ALYA: Yes. Father and Mother would be impressed.

MEENA: Father is waiting at the airport. We've come back to get you. We're going to university!

ALYA: We've never left our village.

MEENA: But the taxi is waiting.

ALYA: There is no taxi.

(ALYA *and* MEENA *regard one another some moments.*)

MEENA: If we were dying, I would remember. I don't remember.

ALYA: But you do. You just don't want to. *(Beat)* What is real is that we are usually hungry. We are usually afraid. We are usually more hungry than afraid for years now. And we don't grow pomegranates anymore. Father sells scraps. Me and you, we can't leave the house so we dream of apples. Of clean water. Of the sweetness of meat and rice.

MEENA: No.

ALYA: We dream of electricity, of our fingers moving on pages, of baskets full for picnics.

MEENA: No.

ALYA: We dream of escaping the Taliban. We dreams of escaping the Americans, of going to England,

MEENA: No.

ALYA: of you and father leaving first, of your coming back to get us.

MEENA: No! It's that simple: to you, Alya, I say no. *(Beat)* Where is my body?

(ALYA *hesitates.*)

MEENA: Where is my body?

(ALYA *points to the medium sandbag.*)

MEENA: That's me?

(ALYA *nods "yes". *MEENA *stands over the bag, looking at it for some moments. Then suddenly she kicks it.*)

MEENA: Get up. (*She kicks it again.*) Get up! (*She kicks it again and again.*) Get up, girl! You will live. You will be a teacher. Do you hear me? You are free now. You will travel. Get up! You will write a brilliant paper on Faiz Ahmed Faiz. Get up! You will kiss a man. Get up. Get up! You will live! You will live!

(MEENA *kicks the bag till she's worn out, then she quits. The three of them are silent some moments.*)

ALYA: It's not your fault, Meena.

MEENA: Why did you let my hand go, Alya? I held on to you so tight, I was afraid I'd break your bones.

ALYA: But I pulled and pulled and finally we came apart. (*She looks at her own hand.*) You used to draw the alphabet on my palm under the table when we sat with the elders. (*Beat*) I'm sorry, Meena.

(ALYA *and* MEENA *are silent some moments.*)

MEENA: It's all right now, hedge hog. Listen. My throat's no longer dry.

(MEENA *now hums the song that* ALYA *hummed earlier.* MEENA *hums it clear and strong.* ALYA *listens with delight. Then the two of them hum the song together. When its over they just stare at each other.*)

SERGIO: How much more time do we got?

ALYA: (*Calmly*) Just a few seconds, I think. I'm going now. I'm the first to go.

(ALYA *approaches* MEENA, *takes her hand and kisses it.*)

ALYA: Meena.

(Then ALYA *releases* MEENA's *hand and takes a sandbag by its corner.* ALYA *begins to drag the sandbag behind her as she exits. But then she stops and looks at the bag, and speaks matter-of-factly.)*

ALYA: Oh. This isn't mine. I'm the small one.

(ALYA now takes hold of the smallest sand bag and drags it away. She glances back once, just for a moment, at MEENA, then disappears off stage. MEENA and SERGIO watch her leave in silence. Then MEENA realizes her sister is truly gone. She calls for her.)

MEENA: Alya? Alya!?

(MEENA listens for a reply. No reply comes.)

SERGIO: Well, I guess I'm next. Damn it's cold. So damn cold.

(SERGIO starts to drag his sandbag back to his bed. MEENA is still watching the place where her sister disappeared. She hears the sound of his sandbag dragging and now regards him.)

MEENA: Soldier.

SERGIO: Yeah?

MEENA: Wherever Joe's place is, you shouldn't have left it.

(SERGIO just looks at MEENA.)

MEENA: Soldier.

SERGIO: Yeah?

MEENA: If you were not dying, I would wish you dead. *(Beat)* Are you sorry?

SERGIO: *(Sincerely)* I wish I had the time to be. *(He drags the sandbag.)*

MEENA: Soldier.

(SERGIO stands still.)

SERGIO: Yeah?

(The following is hard for MEENA *to ask but she makes herself ask it.)*

MEENA: Am I pretty? *(Beat)* Were we pretty? My sister and I.

SERGIO: You were just kids.

MEENA: But if we had grown up?

*(*SERGIO *studies* MEENA *some moments, trying to figure out what she wants. She straightens her shirt, shifts her hair. Then they stare at one another.)*

SERGIO: Well, I wouldn't kicked you out of bed, that's for sure.

MEENA: Bastard. *(Beat)* Thank you.

*(*SERGIO *nods to* MEENA, *then lays the sandbag on his bed as a pillow and lies down on it and closes his eyes. He is shivering badly. She watches him shiver. Then she picks up the burka and nears him. She looks down at him. Then she slowly pulls the burka over him, completely covering him like a shroud. He stops shivering and is still.)*

*(*MEENA *returns to "her" sandbag. She nudges it gently with her foot. No sign of life. She looks around her, sees the suitcase. Calmly, surely, she picks the suitcase up, feeling that it fits well in her hand. Then she stands on the sandbag, holding the suitcase to her chest, readying herself for her journey. She closes her eyes. She hums clearly, strongly, one or two lines of the song she hummed earlier.)*

(Then suddenly MEENA *opens her eyes, no longer humming but looking straight out over the public. Black out)*

END OF PLAY

www.ingramcontent.com/pod-product-compliance
Lightning Source LLC
Chambersburg PA
CBHW070037110426
42741CB00035B/2800